A Child's First Bird Guide

An Interactive Book of Common Birds Found in Eastern North America

Laurina Isabella Lyle, PhD
  Writer | Audio Voice Recording

Karen Black Lyle
  Graphic Artist | Image Editor

Pteris Publishers

Print: 979-8-218-26414-7
Ebook: 979-8-218-26415-4

PterisPublishers
Clarksville, Tennessee

Book Design and Art Work by Karen Black Lyle
Bird Songs recorded by Lang Elliott
Photos from Envato Elements, Adobe Stock

CIP data on file at the Library of Congress

Preface

My interest in birds began at a young age, when I first noticed their remarkable ability to fly while I was stuck on the ground. It was a harsh realization that despite my desire to soar through the air, flying under my own power was something I would never be able to do.

Maybe you have had the same thought.

At school, I asked my science teacher why people couldn't fly. Her answer was simple: we are not physically designed for flight.

That's how it started for me with simple question. From there, I proceeded to learn as much as I could about birds as possible.

Throughout the eastern United States, we witness changing populations of bird species depending on the season of the year. During spring and summer, many of our bird species migrate thousands of miles from southern regions such as Mexico and Central America.

They migrate north to build their homes, lay eggs, and nurture their young. As the end of summer approaches, they spread their wings and fly back south to spend the winter months.

While many birds migrate, there are also some that choose to stay with us all year long. This book delves into the captivating world of 13 year- round residents, offering a glimpse into the field of ornithology - the study of birds.

By familiarizing ourselves with these resident birds, we can gain a solid foundation for further exploration and understanding of our feathered friends.

We wish you the best of luck in discovering them all!

Laurina and Karen

For all children with an eager curiosity to learn about birds.
Dedicated to my grandchildren: Henry, Caroline and Mary Charlotte
Laurina Isabella Lyle

To Mom and Dad for taking me to so many beautiful places outside.
You were right, all trees do not look the same.
Karen Black Lyle

Table of Contents

Getting to know birds in North America.

In this short guide, you will learn how to identify 13 common birds by their look and songs. These feathered creatures can be found in your local area throughout the year, regardless of the season - whether it's spring, summer, fall, or winter. You may spot them in your own backyard, a nearby city park, or a wooded area close to your home.

Learn More

Each two-page spread features one bird in detail. You will discover many helpful pointers for identifying them, as well as fascinating facts about their distinctive habits.

If you want to hear the bird's song or acquire more information, simply point your cell-phone camera at the code. This will direct you to a webpage where you can hear the full melody and learn more.

Don't forget to fill in the date, location, and weather when you first spotted this bird.

Share your new knowledge with friends and family. Good luck with your adventure of seeing and discovering them all.

What is a Bird?

Birds are a group of organisms that look very similar to each other. The reason is because their bodies are shaped to fly.

Here are a few features most birds have in common with each other.

1. They have feathers. Some of their feathers keep them warm, while other feathers help them fly.

2. Birds have a special skeleton that is strong yet light weight.

3. Birds have bills that allow them to eat their food.

4. The legs and feet of birds are covered in scales not feathers.

5. Birds lay eggs.

Can you think of how you are like a bird but not like a bird?

Northern Mockingbird

Mimus polyglottos

ORDER: Passeriformes FAMILY: Mimidae

Mnemonic (sounds like):
Mimics other bird calls, repeats phrases three times, then changes songs.
Scan the code to hear the song and learn more.

ID Tips

Slender bodied, medium-sized gray-brown bird with a black, slightly curved bill. Wings are short compared to a long tail and long legs. Two white wing bars on each wing. When taking flight, a white flash from wings and tail gives them a distinctive appearance.

Habitat Towns	Food Omnivore	Nesting Shrub	Behavior Ground Forager	Conservation Low Concern

The Northern Mockingbird is the Tennessee state bird, as well as seven other states. They are highly intelligent and best known for aggressively defending their territory from intruders. Depending upon the regional location, they can learn over 200 songs of other birds.

Neat Nature for Your Notes

Constantly singing, sometimes at night, Mockingbirds imitate many other birds including the Carolina Wren, Northern Cardinal, and Eastern Bluebird. They also mimic cats, dogs, frogs and even car alarms.

Date spotted _______/_______/_______

Location _____________________

Weather

Think about it

About how many songs can a Mockingbird learn?

American Robin

Turdus migratorius

ORDER: Passeriformes FAMILY: Turdidae

Mnemonic (sounds like):

"Cheer up, Cheerily, Cheerily"

Scan the code to hear the song and learn more.

Habitat	Food	Nesting	Behavior	Conservation
Open Woodlands	Omnivore	Tree	Ground Forager	Low Concern

An easily recognized and common bird found in backyards and woodlands. Robins can be seen running and stopping with their heads cocked looking for insects and earthworms.

Neat Nature for Your Notes

Robin diets vary through the day: more earthworms in the morning and fruit in the afternoon.

Think about it

Have you seen a nest with eggs inside?

Date spotted ______/______/______

Location ______________________

Weather    

Carolina Chickadee

Poecile carolinensis

ORDER: Passeriformes FAMILY: Paridae

Mnemonic (sounds like):

"Chick'adee-dee-dee"

Scan the code to hear the song and learn more.

Habitat
Forests

Food
Omnivore

Nesting
Cavity

Behavior
Foliage Gleaner

LOW

Conservation
Low Concern

During the winter, Carolina Chickadees flock together. Each member of the flock has a rank; the highest-ranking individuals will mate the next spring.

Neat Nature for Your Notes

The Carolina chickadee communicates complex alarm messages to the whole woodland. The more "dees" it adds to the call, the greater the danger. If an owl or hawk is flying above, the bird will call a quiet "seet" and life in the forest freezes.

Date spotted ______/______/______

Location ______________________

Weather

Think about it

What are some ways your community warns you about danger?

Blue Jay

Impossible to miss the prominent crest and blue. white. and black plumage.

Cyanocitta cristata

ORDER: Passeriformes FAMILY: Corvidae

Mnemonic (sounds like):

"Jay"

Scan the code to hear the song and learn more.

Habitat	Food	Nesting	Behavior	Conservation
Forests	Omnivore	Tree	Ground Forager	Low Concern

This large, common and noisy songbird is highly intelligent.

Neat Nature for Your Notes

Jays are partial to eating acorns. In fact, they are credited with helping to spread oak trees after the last glacial period. The next oak tree you see might have been planted by a Blue Jay.

Date spotted ______/______/______

Location ____________________

Weather

Think about it

Do you know that you too can plant trees to help the woodlands?

Eastern Bluebird

ID Tips

Males are a vivid blue with a brick red colored throat and breast. Females are grayish with bluish wings and light orange breasts.

Sialis sialis

ORDER: Passeriformes FAMILY: Turdidae

Mnemonic (sounds like):

"Cheer, Cheerful, Charmer"

Scan the code to hear the song and learn more.

				LOW
Habitat Grasslands	**Food** Omnivore	**Nesting** Cavity	**Behavior** Ground Forager	**Conservation** Low Concern

A small thrush between the size of a Chickadee and a Robin. Bluebirds can be seen flitting from nesting box to perch on nearby snags, and then dropping onto the ground for insects.

Neat Nature for Your Notes

Join the Bluebird Society and help in maintaining the Bluebird population.

Think about it

How does a baby bird get food?

Date spotted ______/______/______

Location __________________

Weather    

Tufted Titmouse

ID Tips

A small. silvery gray bird with a crest. black forehead. and large dark eyes.

Baeolophus bicolor

ORDER: Passeriformes FAMILY: Paridae

Mnemonic (sounds like):

"Peter, Peter, Peter"

Scan the code to hear the song and learn more.

Habitat
Forests

Food
Omnivore

Nesting
Cavity

Behavior
Foliage Gleaner

LOW

Conservation
Low Concern

A very vocal and acrobatic bird. About the same size as a Carolina Chickadee, they are often in the company of other small birds.

Neat Nature for Your Notes

Unable to excavate their own nests, they take advantage of tree cavities of old nests made by woodpeckers. They then line their nests with leaves, moss and grasses and finish it off with an inner layer of hair gathered from mammals such as squirrels, raccoons, and even dogs.

Date spotted ______/______/______

Location ____________________

Weather

Think about it

Can you say tufted titmouse three tmes quickly?

Carolina Wren

Thryothorus ludovicianus

ORDER: Passeriformes FAMILY: Troglodytidae

Mnemonic (sounds like):

"Teakettle, Teakettle, Teakettle"

Scan the code to hear the song and learn more.

Habitat	Food	Nesting	Behavior	Conservation
Open Woodlands	Omnivore	Cavity	Ground Forager	Low Concern

A small, sparrow sized bird with a big sound. Keeping to dense vegetation, it is more readily heard than seen.

Neat Nature for Your Notes

Even though more difficult to see than the other birds in this guide, you are likely to hear the Carolina Wren as it assertively defends its territory by constantly singing.

Think about it

Have you ever seen a bird house?

Date spotted ______/______/______

Location ________________________

Weather

Northern Cardinal

ID Tips

Males are bright red while females are pale olive brown with tinges of red on their feathers and crests. Both have a sturdy orange colored bill.

Cardinalis cardinalis

ORDER: Passeriformes FAMILY: Cardinalidae

Mnemonic (sounds like):

"What Cheer, What Cheer"

Scan the code to hear the song and learn more.

Habitat
Open Woodlands

Food
Seeds

Nesting
Shrub

Behavior
Ground Forager

LOW

Conservation
Low Concern

This large brilliant red crested bird with a black mask is impossible to miss. Cardinals don't molt into a dull plumage during the winter. "What Cheer, What Cheer!" they bring to a gray day in winter.

Neat Nature for Your Notes

Cardinals are aggressive and territorial during mating season. They can be seen squabbling with their own reflections on car mirrors, glass, or other reflective surfaces.

Date spotted ______/______/______

Location ____________________

Weather

Think about it

How do cardinals bring cheer during winter?

Eastern Towhee

Pipilo erythrophthalmus

ORDER: Passeriformes FAMILY: Passerellidae

Mnemonic (sounds like):

"Drink Your Teee"

Scan the code to hear the song and learn more.

ID Tips

Considered a large sparrow. its tri-coloration distinguishes the Towhee from other birds. Males have a black head. throat. and upper body. The sides are orange with a white belly. Females are brown instead of black.

Habitat
Shrub

Food
Omnivore

Nesting
Ground

Behavior
Ground Forager

Conservation
Low Concern

A robin-sized bird of the undergrowth, the Towhee can be heard rummaging around in the leaf litter.

Neat Nature for Your Notes

The Brown-headed Cowbird often parasitizes Eastern Towhee nests. Female Towhees are unable to tell the difference between her own eggs and that of the Cowbird. She will raise the hatchling as her own.

Date spotted ______/______/______

Location ____________________

Weather

Think about it

Are you an omnivore? Do you eat many different types of food?

Wild Turkey

Meleagris gallopavo

ORDER: Galliformes FAMILY: Phasianidae

Mnemonic (sounds like):

"Gobble, Gobble, Gobble"

Scan the code to hear the song and learn more.

The males have a naked red-and-blue head with a wattle. When displaying for females, males expand their tail feathers into a fan. Females are also large, but lack the turkey fan and brightly colored head.

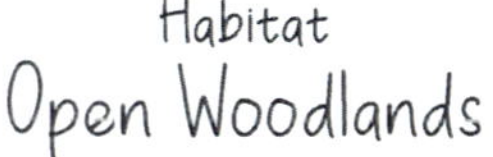

Habitat
Open Woodlands

Food
Omnivore

Nesting
Ground

Behavior
Ground Forager

LOW

Conservation
Low Concern

A very large game bird that has made an incredible comeback after a drastic decline. They have now returned to all 48 states in the continental United States.

Neat Nature for Your Notes

Turkeys can swim by streamlining their bodies into a duck shape and kicking with their feet.

Date spotted _______/_______/_______

Location ___________________________

Weather

Think about it

Did you know that wild turkeys build their nests on the ground?

Pileated Woodpecker

The largest woodpecker is the size of a crow. Both males and females share the bright red crest and black body. Only the male has a red stripe on its cheek.

Dryocopus pileatus

ORDER: Piciformes FAMILY: Picidae

Mnemonic (sounds like):

"Kik, Kik, Kik"

Scan the code to hear the song and learn more.

Habitat	Food	Nesting	Behavior	Conservation
Forests	Omnivore	Cavity	Bark Gleaner	Low Concern

Looking like a flying dinosaur, these striking birds own the forest with their loud calls.

Neat Nature for Your Notes

A sure sign that a Pileated Woodpecker is whacking on a tree is telltale rectangular shaped holes in the bark. Like a bird buffet, other species of birds know that these holes signal a free meal of ants and grubs.

Think about it

Have you heard a woodpecker hammering on a tree?

Date spotted ______/______/______

Location ____________________

Weather    

Barred Owl

ID Tips

A rounded head. no ear tufts. and medium length. rounded tail with large brown eyes. and a yellow bill. The body is a mottled brown with vertical stripes on the under parts.

Strix varia

ORDER: **Strigiformes** FAMILY: **Strigidae**

Mnemonic (sounds like):

"Who Cooks for You? Who Cooks for You All?"

Scan the code to hear the song and learn more.

Habitat
Forests

Food
Mammals

Nesting
Tree

Behavior
Aerial Dive

LOW
Conservation
Low Concern

The Barred Owl is a silent nocturnal watcher in the forest. Listen from your sit spot and you might hear this magnificent bird.

Neat Nature for Your Notes

As home bodies, Barred Owls not only forego migrating but prefer to stay close to home ranging no more than a few miles. When you hear the familiar call, "Who cooks for you?" try mimicking the call which just might result in an owl-eyed investigatation.

Think about it

Why are owls so quiet when they glide through the forest?

Date spotted _____/_____/_____

Location ______________________

Weather

American Goldfinch

Spinus tristis

ORDER: Passeriformes   FAMILY: Fringillidae

Mnemonic (sounds like):

"Per-chik'-o-ree" "Babeee"

Scan the code to hear the song and learn more.

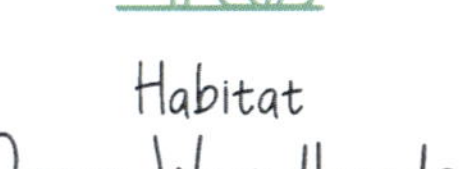

Habitat	Food	Nesting	Behavior	Conservation
Open Woodlands	Seeds	Shrub	Foliage Gleaner	LOW Low Concern

This small finch with a short conical bill is found in weedy fields with thistles and asters. They are an easy bird to photograph for an award-winning picture.

Neat Nature for Your Notes

Goldfinches are the strictest vegetarians in the bird world. While Brown-headed Cowbirds may parasitize Goldfinches, the cowbird hatchlings seldom survive on their vegetarian diet.

Date spotted ______/______/______

Location ________________________

Weather

Think about it

Do you know you can help birds by putting out a bird feeder?

Helpful Tips to Start:

1. Begin with what you know and build your bird and nature knowledge from there.

2. Find a "sit spot" in the park where you can quietly observe and listen.

3. Start a nature notebook to record what you see and hear.

4. Carry Binoculars.

5. Download FREE Apps like, "iNaturalist," "Merlin Bird ID," and "eBird" to your cell phone.

6. Join Audubon for Kids, online resource for kids to learn more about birds with fun activities and so much more. *www.audubon.org/get-outside/activities/audubon-for-kids*

Parts of a Bird

www.ingramcontent.com/pod-product-compliance
Lightning Source LLC
Chambersburg PA
CBRC090747110726
48005CB00008B/990